TINY
YouTube

The ultimate guide to starting, growing & making money from your small YouTube channel

RealToughCandy

Copyright © 2019 by RealToughCandy

All rights reserved. No part of this publication may be reproduced, distributed, or transmitted in any form or by any means, including photocopying, recording, or other electronic or mechanical methods, without the prior written permission of the publisher, except in the case of brief quotations embodied in critical reviews and certain other noncommercial uses permitted by copyright law.

First Edition

www.realtoughcandy.com

CONTENTS

Copyright	
CONTENTS	
Preface	1
Introduction	4
Part I: Building Your Channel	6
Your YouTube Game Plan	7
Choosing a Niche	16
The Tech Flow	21
YouTube 2.0: Content Creation	31
Part II: Making Money	51
Channel Monetization	53
Affiliate Marketing	56
Self-Produced Goods and Services	59
Blog	63
Sponsorships	66
Subscriber Advertising	73
Donations	77
Conclusion	80
Appendix A: New YouTuber Questions	81
Appendix B: Sample Sponsorship Proposal Email	86

"Our greatest weakness lies in giving up. The most certain way to succeed is always to try just one more time"

-THOMAS EDISON

PREFACE

I started my first YouTube channel in 2011. Stationed overseas as an enlisted airman in the Air Force, I had just dropped an electro-funk EP and wanted to share my music with the world. So, I did what any other self-respecting indie musician does: I found a free video editor, threw down a few tracks next to some stock zombie footage and got to uploading.

Since then, I've had a few different channels that featured a variety of material, from vinyl collecting to kombucha reviews, and even a local weekly news program I produced.

But by 2016, things had changed. While I enjoyed making videos for the world, I also spent a lot of time on it. Not only that, a lot of videos featured some pretty valuable insider information! For example, I did videos on how to properly ship a vinyl record and how to sell vintage items on eBay with competitive pricing. I felt like I was ready to go to the next level, but things were so unfocused. How would I get an audience? I didn't know a lot of movers and shakers online, so who would spread the word? What would I even produce so that people would care? The 15 views on my *Law and Order: SVU* earrings review was exciting, but I knew I could do better...Especially because 10 of those views were mine.

Finally, in the spring of 2016, after a string of thoroughly random video uploads (a beer review, a how-to-configure-a-VPN tutorial, and a tasteless satire video on Minnesota Governor Mark Dayton published the same week), I decided to reframe my 20-subscriber channel and present my newest passion to the world: software development. Specifically, web development. Sure, I'd lose most of those subscribed to me but what did I really have to lose?

Since I was still in my learning phase as a software newbie, most of those early tech videos involved me complaining about something out of frustration. As a self-taught developer, there's a lot to be frustrated about. It's a tough career field and there's **so** much to learn.

Fascinatingly, one of my rant videos ended up getting over 20,000 views in its first few months of existence. I was floored! That video alone ended up earning me over $100 in Google AdSense ad revenue. The irony was, once I started progressing in my career, I pulled most of those older videos because they were pretty bad. Regardless, that was my first signal that a person could make money doing YouTube, even if she didn't have many subscribers: I had under 1000 subs when that video blew up.

As a software developer, coding things is my day job and it's also part of my YouTube job where I share software-related topics with the world.

But some nights I want to explore something different. I have no idea how I end up on these topics, but sometimes I'll be browsing on YouTube and stumble upon some really...*interesting* channels. Channels that sometimes make me say, "Wow, really? People tune into this stuff?" It's not your typical bodybuilding or longer-lashes beauty tutorial, but weirder stuff like live chicken cams. That's right, a 24/7 live feed of chickens just doing their thing. No doubt you've also stumbled across some of these channels.

You might be surprised to hear some of the things people watch on YouTube, but you might even be *more* surprised to learn that there's an audience for what **you** do.

Maybe you absolutely love cats.

Maybe you struggle with mental illness and want to share your journey.

Maybe you're in a career field you find interesting.

Whatever you find interest in, you're able to turn into a channel. We'll talk all about that in a dedicated chapter, but for now just keep it in the back of your mind that nearly *anything* can be turned into a money-making YouTube channel.

You don't have to have a million subscribers to make money with YouTube. **Far from it.** Aside from showing you how to develop a sustainable, high-quality channel, in this book I'm also going to share with you the secrets for making money with it -- whether you have ten subscribers or 5,000. The knowledge I share in this book is directly influenced by my experiences from my own my small YouTube channel, which at publication time has less than 10,000 subscribers.

So, whether you're trying to go full-time YouTube or just want some pocket money at the end of the month, this book can help you get there.

The type of channel I'm trying to help you build is one that will offer loads of value to an eager audience, from "super-subscribers" who comment on every video to the lurkers who stay in the shadows (yet just can't get enough of your material). Success comes a *lot* easier when people like what you do!

This approach allows you to earn income while growing your channel, and you'll be able to integrate sustainable practices that will pave the way for your channel's continuous growth. Now... Let's go build a great YouTube channel.

INTRODUCTION

This book is separated into two sections.

The first section deals with organizing your YouTube channel if you don't have one yet. If you *do* have a channel, you can still learn a lot from this section since we discuss building and keeping an audience; there's no such thing as too much audience engagement!

In that section we'll also focus on the bigger-picture stuff that the YouTube Help pages don't really provide: things like developing a game plan, choosing a niche, SEO, developing a technical workflow, and more. All of these things are going to set you up for finding an audience and getting monetized.

In the second section, I show you how to start earning. Even if it's not your primary goal as a YouTuber, these are your main options for being compensated for your hard work. Take advantage! There are seven avenues I discuss for generating income and each of them gets their own chapter: Channel monetization, affiliate marketing, self-produced goods and services, blog, sponsorships, subscriber & peer advertising, and donations.

There's also a New YouTuber Questions appendix, where I address things like giveaways, trolls, sub-4-sub schemes and shy personalities.

But before we do anything crazy, Chapter 1 sets the mood. We're going to do some serious thinking and ask challenging questions about your goals for your channel. What do you want out of your channel: A platform to share knowledge with the world? A chance to build community? A place to help people make better decisions? A date? There's no wrong answer to this, but it's important you identify what truly motivates you because it'll allow you to create relevant content that both you *and* your audience enjoy.

"But Candy, I didn't ask for the lecture on planning. I want to get subscribers, make awesome videos and make some dang money!" I know how eager you are to get rolling with that! But it's **so** important to have a plan before proceeding—otherwise you're just floating from video to video, hoping something will go right.

Hoping somebody influential will share your latest vid.

Hoping the algorithm will pick you up.

Hoping something will just….happen with that *Law and Order: SVU* earring review.

The first year of my channel was like that and it was neither financially fruitful nor mentally satisfying.

So, instead of *hoping* to grow, we're going to do some ***planning*** for your growth.

Ready? Let's do this.

PART I: BUILDING YOUR CHANNEL

Welcome to Part I of the book where we focus on building a sustainable channel that both you and your audience enjoy. With **value** as a guiding principle, by the end of this section you'll not only have a YouTube game plan, but you'll also have a grasp on choosing a niche, technical workflows, and content creation.

YOUR YOUTUBE GAME PLAN

Here's what's awesome about YouTube: anyone can press the big red record button on their camera, sign in to YouTube and publish videos for the world to see. In fact, millions of people on YouTube do just that. But in order to succeed as a small YouTuber – one that consistently engages community members and provides value – we'll need to go above and beyond the basic requirements and bring our A game. We'll start by thinking about the value we can offer.

Value: The Cornerstone of All Successful YouTube Channels

What is value?

We normally equate value with something like getting a good deal at the grocery store or when booking a hotel. We equate **value** with getting a **deal**.

"Oh, gallons of milk are two for five bucks right now? That's a good value!"

"I just booked two nights in Vegas at the MGM for $100! Somebody pass me my lucky rabbit's foot and suntan lotion. What a steal!"

But when it comes to offering value to your audience, the definition of value is a lot more expansive. Just like art is in the eye of the beholder, so is value in this case. For example, you may produce videos on betta fish swimming around. No commentary; no educational component: just hours and hours of a camera focused on your fish tank. Who would ever want to watch that, amirite?

But there's value in these seemingly snooze-worthy videos. There are thousands of people out there who will find peacefulness in the gently-bubbling water, the calming lights, and the gracefulness of the swimming fish. Some will play the video while trying to fall asleep or needing to decompress after a hard day's work. That modest camera capturing a tiny aquatic creature just added massive value to many peoples' day. It may be hard to imagine, especially if fish aren't your thing. But a video just as I described is well on its way to 100,000 views and has dozens of comments! It's called Halfmoon Betta Fish ~ Hikki Chan (HD).

The thing about value is that you don't have to be a mattress liquidator or a grocery store selling Lil' Smokies at wholesale prices to provide value.

Maybe your audience just needs a quick laugh.

Maybe you have insider tips on a career field that people are just dying to know about.

Maybe they are craving five hours of Balinese Gamelan music.

The point is, it could be something mainstream or totally out there, but *your audience determines value.* That's why it's so important to become engaged with them, research and study them, and respect them along with their ideas and opinions. If you **can't** add value to their lives with your videos, you'll end up at the bottom of the YouTube heap and they'll find value somewhere else.

You can Google and research a topic for hours, crunch the numbers, be on fleek with your title and thumbnail, and have a fascinating pinned comment, but at the essence of your YouTube career is *providing value.*

So now you understand that value is at the front and center of any successful YouTube channel, big or small. Great, but now what? Let's go get some ideas for our channel from the wild world of YouTube.

Try this:

Identify a handful of channels you enjoy – channels you could see yourself producing or would like to *eventually* see yourself producing. Don't worry if the production values are out of your league, the host is a total hottie with a 10-person makeup team and a pet chinchilla that uses Aquanet, or any other component that seems far away from your current reality. Identify things you think are cool, things that this person is doing differently to stand out from the pack.

Go to their video page and sort their videos by "Most popular." What topics are big hits with viewers? Does this person have viral videos in their collection? What year were they produced and what made them go viral: what did the thumbnail look like, what did the title say, what was the run time? Did the creator respond to any comments? Take notes on all this.

Also identify things that *aren't* so great that you want to avoid in your own productions. What are commenters saying about the video and the person hosting it? Does the mic suck? Is the video only available in 360p or lower resolution?

From the description, to the pinned comment, to the thumbnail to the video itself, write down the winning elements, concepts, and topics you can incorporate into your own channel, along with the not-so-hot things you want to avoid. Let's take it one step further.

Ready...Set...Start stealing!

Want to know a fast way to greatness? Start stealing! Wait, what? That's not exactly a technique you picked up in high school shop class.

To clarify: there's *good* stealing and then there's *bad* stealing.

Good stealing is when you find ideas that you like and make them your own. There's no law against it, nearly everybody does it in one way or another, and it helps make you a better creator.

On the other hand, there's **bad** stealing. Bad stealing is when you blatantly rip-off a person's ideas or styles, not bothering to give them credit, and then use and claim those ideas and styles as their own. Never, under any circumstance, go through with bad stealing! Peoples' careers are ruined all the time for plagiarism, and besides, YouTubers aren't coming to your channel so they can watch Logan Paul, h3h3Productions, or FBE. They can just as easily log on to the **real** Logan Paul, h3h3Productions and FBE channels.

Remember, half of YouTube's name is still *You*: people want to hear, see, and otherwise experience **you**, regardless if you have butt implants or not. People want **you**, whether you have 100 or 100 million subscribers. This is the case even with highly technical channels, or even channels where you don't show your face. Your voice, your way of producing videos, and your overall tone are all going to be things that bring people back to your channel time and time again.

It's very easy to fall into the YouTube trap where you see channels doing ridiculous pranks and makeup tutorials racking up millions of views. And hey, maybe you love doing ridiculous pranks or makeup tuts. But for those of us who don't, it's critically important to focus on what **you** enjoy. Because if you're chasing something you don't like, you may as well go back to the normal world to work for somebody else, toiling away on somebody else's dream. That's a lot easier than doing YouTube as a clone -- plus the money is definitely more consistent with a 9-5 job. It's tempting to try and be someone you're not in order to rack up views and presumably more income opportunities, but it's just not worth it.

It's a trap.

Stay true to yourself and you will gain more of everything: subscribers, respect, video shares, earnings.

Your Goals and Purpose as a YouTuber (do not skip)

I would see sections like this in books and always skip them: *"What are my **goals**? What is my **purpose**? Pure fluff, gimme the protein!"*

But in order to have a successful and sustainable channel, you need to identify your goals. Even if you don't know your niche yet, you probably know what you want out of your channel. Maybe you want to build a platform to share knowledge with the world? Perhaps finding community and building an online social group is important to you. Or are you more of the benevolent type, and want to help people make better decisions? Are you looking for love? Is your primary goal to make money? As mentioned earlier, there's no wrong answer to this, but you **must** identify what truly motivates you. Understanding your goals and purpose will allow you to create relevant content that both you *and* your audience enjoy. Really take some time with this one because it's going to flavor the tone and trajectory of your channel.

Tech Tools for Video Making

YouTube is abundant with content and sometimes creators think they need the best camera, mic, or special effects to really make their channel blow up. That couldn't be further from the truth. Viewers know they're not in an IMAX theatre, so they're not normally expecting mind-blowing video production. That said, there are a few minimum standards you'll need to fulfill, like 1080p video resolution, a clear voice, and non-super-shaky video.

Fortunately, you probably have most of the tools that achieve these standards around your house somewhere -- and if you don't, you don't have to break the bank. You'll need a camera, computer, software, microphone, and headphones.

Camera

There are many decent cameras out there for less than $200 (even less used). For example, the Canon PowerShot ELPH 360 is less than $200 new and boasts numerous features including 1080p HD capabilities; built-in WiFi; and a 20.2 MP CMOS sensor with DIGIC 4+ Image Processor (camera nerd speak for: it creates really crispy images even in low lighting situations).

Because camera companies are continuously cranking out new models, just Google "best cheap camera for YouTube" and you'll have plenty of options to choose from.

For my own videos, I have an older (2007-ish) Nikon D7000 I previously used when I did "stand-ups" (me on camera). Back in the day I would just plug in a cheap but functional lavalier mic, sit near my my fireplace and talk to the camera about tech topics. These days I use my smartphone for stand-ups or outdoor scenes and apply color correction as needed using editing software.

The big benefit with phones is that you can also edit and upload videos on them – a one-stop-shop for YouTubing. The YouTube Creator Academy has some useful basic pointers for shooting on a phone.

Computer

Video editing is a resource hog and you may find your normal computer getting a little cranky when you start editing video clips. For any major video editing program I recommend at least 16GB of RAM, and 30GB of free space on your hard drive. If you want to keep your archival videos/footage, check out portable hard drive options (I use 1TB USB LaCie drives).

Video Recording Software

You don't need any special software when recording with a camera or smartphone, but screencasts can be done for free using the open-source OBS application. This is an excellent program with numerous options for screencasts, plus live streaming capabilities. I use OBS exclusively for my YouTube screencasts (which are most of my videos) and have always had great results.

Video Editing Software

Desktop options for video editing:

- Adobe Premiere Pro (paid, Windows & Mac)
- Sony Vegas Pro (paid, Windows)
- Final Cut Pro (paid, Mac)
- Lightworks (free and paid tiers, Windows, Mac & Linux)
- Blender (free, Windows, Mac & Linux [best for 3d animation])
- Shotcut (free, Windows, Mac & Linux)
- OpenShot (free, Linux)
- Kdenlive (free, Linux)

There are many others, but these are some good ones to start researching. My personal choices are Premiere Pro & Sony Vegas Pro for Windows, Final Cut Pro for Mac, and Kdenlive for Linux. If you're an Apple product user, you've probably seen iMovie on your machine. I don't recommend this program as it's very basic, only supporting two video tracks along with many other limitations. However, it could be a good training program to get you familiar with the basic editing process.

Desktop screencasting:

- OBS (open source; available for Windows, Mac and Linux)

Mobile iOS editors:

- Mobile Fusion (paid)

Android editors:
- Kinemaster (free & paid tiers)

Cross-platform mobile editors:
- Adobe Premiere Rush (paid)

Microphone

While you can use your laptop's built-in mic in a pinch, upgrading to a decent external microphone can be done for $100 or less. The problem with relying on internal computer mics is that they capture a lot of ambient noise and hiss. Many times if you try to solve this problem by getting really close to it, you risk distortion.

The Blue Yeti line is perhaps the best-known and most reliable line on the market for YouTubers. They're a breeze to install and start using, especially with the built-in USB capability. There's no driver to install with these mics; just plug and play. Their Nano Premium model is currently under $99 on Amazon and has killer reviews.

For on-the-go recording and some smartphone situations, you may find a lavalier mic the better option. This is a small, clip-on style mic that attaches to your shirt. Lavalier mics are inexpensive and as the cheaper option don't have the controls that "desktop" or condenser mics have. You simply plug it into your camera or smartphone (usually via the 3.5mm jack) and go.

Headphones

You should always test your audio from your computer's speakers in addition to a pair of headphones, especially if you're mixing dialogue with music. Your headphones don't have to be fancy and can be picked up at any thrift store for a few bucks if you're on a budget.

If you have some money to spare, Sennheiser's HD280PRO model are hands-down the best headphones I've used under $100. As a musician, I've used a lot of headphones over the years but these have been absolute beasts whether I'm monitoring music videos, recording podcasts, or editing sound clips. Try to avoid headphones that have built-in EQ or bass boosters (Beats by Dre, SkullCandy Crusher, etc.); you'll want something that more accurately represents the EQ in your audio tracks.

Summary

In this section you had a chance to develop your own vision for your channel. You also learned that value is a cornerstone concept when it comes to developing a channel that grabs subscribers and keeps them coming back. Finally, we went over the basic gear list for getting started with quality video production without being excessive. Now let's talk about what kinds of videos you're going to make.

CHOOSING A NICHE

You probably have interests in a lot of things. From video games to exercise to animals to friends to parties to going out...The list is indeed endless with what we enjoy about life. But with the YouTube game it's critical to pick a speciality, or *niche,* so your audience knows what to expect. After all, it's the reason they click "Subscribe" in the first place — they want to see more of what you did in a particular video. Picking a niche may be super obvious for you, or you might be torn in which direction to go. Fear not, because this section deals exclusively with discovering a niche that's a great fit for you.

Fortunately, we can make the niche-selection process a little easier by using four guiding concepts consisting of **Personal Interest, Demand, Competition,** and **Purpose.**

Wait...no "Passion" in that list?

It's true. But hear me out: How many times have you heard people say "You need to have passion to truly succeed" or "Do what you're passionate about?"

Probably a lot. Well, I don't believe you have to be passionate to succeed. In my experience, passion is something you love sooooo much that you don't care if you get paid or not: you do it for the love.

Do I really enjoy software and web development? **Yes**.

Am I *passionate* about it? **No.**

Software development is something that's allowed me to succeed in the modern world but I'm definitely not losing sleep over the fact that JavaScript was just dethroned as the world's top programming language. I'm not doing slam poetry about HTTP requests and I'm definitely not organizing a protest over the decline of Perl's popularity over the last two decades. This is all to say that *it's OK if you chose a niche that you're not passionate about.* The far more important thing is that you have a personal interest in your niche.

Personal Interest

Having a personal interest in your niche is important for a few reasons:

- You're going to be making hundreds or thousands of videos centering on this concept. Burnout comes faster when you aren't interested in doing something yet feel an obligation to do it.
- It keeps you interested and people sense the excitement: when you're bored or disengaged, so are your viewers.
- A personal interest in your niche keeps your channel in business. It's easier to walk away when you don't have a personal interest and things go wrong.

Sure, there are plenty of niches/topics that pay better ad rates or seemingly attract bigger audiences. But if you're just making videos on a topic to feed the machine, you may as well just get some more hours in at your day job. Choose a niche you have a personal interest in and you'll be happier. You'll be more engaged with your subscribers. And, you'll *always* have video ideas bubbling up.

You may have a niche that popped right into your head — great! If you're juggling a few niches or still don't have one in mind, the next three guiding concepts will help you get more organized.

Purpose

Now that you probably have some niche ideas, think about why you're doing the channel in the first place. For example, let's say your niche is duck hunting.

Are you going to be primarily an entertainment channel, bringing the camera out to your favorite spots while having some fun? Will you offer educational videos, like what to look for when selecting a good boat? Will you do tutorials, rants, insider vids? Or will you be an all-encompassing destination channel doing all of the above?

You can always adjust your video styles according to your audience, so it's OK if you don't have an answer right away, but start thinking of some video ideas you can start your channel off within this niche. Don't fuss with researching the demand for these topics at the moment; the important part is to write down all of your ideas. You can mold the rough idea into a finely-tuned, SEO-friendly topic later in the process.

Going back to the duck hunting channel example, let's say you've decided to be a destination channel for all things duck hunting. Some rough but strong video ideas might be:

- why do you need a duck boat
- duck recipes
- Best duck hunting camo
- Best times to go duck hunting
- successful duck hunting & weather misconceptions

Demand

Now it's time to see if people are actually tuning in to your ideas. Are people searching for this topic, or something similar to it, on Google and YouTube? (We'll go over some great tools to help you with this in the next chapter). To be fair, you don't have to conform to what people are currently searching -- maybe your ideas are so avant-garde or original that nobody has done what you're doing yet -- but it's difficult to gain traction early on as a completely-original, going-against-the-system YouTuber.

One alternative to that would be to choose a proven niche (i.e. a niche with topics that people are searching for), then weave in your original ideas into the production of the videos. Life doesn't have to be cookie cutter, thank goodness, but you've definitely got to get butts into the seats before you can make an impact with your videos.

Competition

What are other people in your niche doing? If a popular YouTuber in your niche is wearing a golden retriever costume while playing Duck Hunt, does that inspire you or make you cringe? By studying your potential niche's competition, you can get a better idea on how you want to run your own channel.

But what about a lot of competitors who have seemingly taken all the good topics? Time to find a new niche, right? No way. Consider this theoretical situation: While researching your competition on Google, you plug in your own video ideas and see that others have already published similar blog posts and videos. It may be tempting to shy away from topics already covered or even ditch the niche, but most likely these are topics a lot of people are also searching for. In other words, there's demand for the topic.

But how do you become competitive and start siphoning off some of that sweet traffic when these people are already established and you're just starting out? The easiest way is to one-up them. For example, if your competition did a video titled "4 Signs You Need a Duck Boat" you could do a video on the **five** signs you need a duck boat. If somebody did a video on their 10 all-time favorite duck recipes, do a video on your **15** all-time favorite duck recipes. If a blogger published a post in 2017 titled "Best Times to Go Duck Hunting in the Midwest," do your video on the best times to go duck hunting in the Midwest **in 2019**.

Referencing the current year in your video and video title can almost always be used to your advantage when it comes to a topic that is heavily covered in your niche -- most web content has a very limited shelf life, so this gives you an opportunity to swoop in and take the lead.

So the new idea list could be something like this:

- 5 signs you need a duck boat
- 15 all-time favorite duck recipes
- Best duck hunting camo manufacturers for 2019
- Best times to go duck hunting in the Midwest (2019)
- 4 huge duck hunting weather misconceptions

To summarize, choosing a niche is essential for your success as a YouTuber. It helps keep you focused, it turns viewers into subscribers, and it makes your job as a YouTuber so much easier.

Personal Interest, Demand, Competition, and Purpose all come into play when choosing a great niche for you and your channel. You don't have to have passion for your niche to succeed, but you do need to have an interest in it. Similarly, your niche should be something that people search for, your purpose in your niche should be somewhat clear, and you should explore the competition in your niche to get a feel for its overall flavor and tone to help guide your own niche-related choices.

THE TECH FLOW

Video planning, recording, editing & publishing

You've decided on a niche and you're motivated to start making videos. Awesome! One problem though...What videos are you actually going to produce? How and where are you going to produce them? When will you publish them? In this chapter, we're setting up a workflow so that your channel resembles a humming, well-oiled machine. As a result, you'll have more time, more energy, and more channel engagement. In this chapter we're discussing video planning, recording, editing, and publishing your YouTube masterpieces. Finally, we go over some valuable browser extensions like Keywords Everywhere and vidIQ to help you make discoverable, engaging videos.

Video planning

Getting into the groove with planning your videos is paramount in your success as a YouTuber. It's going to be the critical component that separates you from the rest of the pack. Most YouTubers, and even many who are trying to earn money from YouTube, take a nonchalant approach, cranking out videos when the mood strikes with no rhyme or reason.

Good video planning takes many variables into consideration including your audience demographics, your niche, your other life activities, and so much more. Like other components of your channel, we'll start with the simple and low-hanging fruit: upload frequency.

Upload Frequency

One thing you can do right away before you even decide on video topics is to get an idea of your upload frequency. Are you a vlogger who can handle daily videos where the content flows fast and cheap with no editing required? Get ready for a wild ride with a fast tempo. Are you comfortable with a Monday-Wednesday-Friday routine? Or do you prefer a few videos a week but not sure what days work best? Whatever you decide on, pencil this number into your video production plan because it's not only going to guide you as a creator, but this schedule also lets your audience know what to expect.

For me, my subscribers can expect at least one video a week and anything else is a bonus. Sometimes I do daily videos, sometimes three videos a week, but the baseline is at least one a week. Establish your own baseline, stick to it, and modify if necessary. I recommend doing at least one video a week to keep your audience engaged -- anything less you run the risk of getting your videos and your entire channel lost in the shuffle. Remember, when people can't engage with you, they will absolutely find it somewhere else. Don't get lost in the mix with infrequent, inconsistent uploads.

Video Topics: What Kinds of Videos Will I Produce?

You've picked your niche earlier on, which now dramatically reduces the stress of operating a YouTube channel: instead of literally a million topics to choose from, you've narrowed it down to a few hundred, give or take. Great! But now what?

Start by simply writing down some topics and styles in your niche that you find interesting. Whether they're instructional or how-to videos, reviews, commentary, screencasts, vlogs, or something else, these are going to be the springboard topics and styles for your big debut so write down as many as you can. Just like in the last chapter when establishing the purpose of your channel, don't worry about whether or not people are searching for these topics right now. That can come later. The important thing is to get all your ideas written down.

Once you look over them, there'll probably be a few topics that are of particular interest to you. Your enthusiasm plays a big part in the success of a video (especially your earliest ones), so highlight three to five video ideas/topics from this list. Take a few minutes to envision how you might produce this video and deliver the message. Answer these questions:

- What images, video clips, or text will complement this video?
- What key points will I cover; what message will I deliver?
- What's the tone of this message?
- How are my viewers going to benefit from this video?
- What will my intro and conclusion sound like?
- Will there be music in the background to set the mood? What kind?
- Will I be on camera, will something else be on camera or is this more suitable for a screencast?

Take a few minutes to let the movie in your mind guide you; storyboard the idea if necessary. Planning a video is just like planning a book -- remember those book outlines you had to do in 7th grade and then again in college? It's the same idea with videos. You could even use a book outline template to structure the content of your video if it helps you visualize things.

To Script or Not to Script

Some creators script their videos, others don't. The benefits of scripting is that once you write out what you want to say, it eliminates a lot of video editing time because you're not fumbling for words, getting sidetracked, or fluffing the air with verbal pauses. You can also easily convert your script into a blog post with a few easy edits.

However, it does take practice to sound natural when reading from a script, so give it some practice runs if you decide on the scripted route. Remember, your audience came to hear **you** speak rather than a human screen-reader. If you're having trouble bridging the gap between reading from a script and sounding natural, try starting off with some bullet points or notes. You could also do a portion of your video with a script, like the intro, then transition into the "protein" of your video with notes, bullet points, or even completely ad-libbed.

I like scripting because it saves time in the editing process and it lets me convey a message with surgical precision. However, it does take time to write a script and so I'll usually script my intro to grab peoples' attention, then ad-lib my talking points and edit out the nonsense in Final Cut Pro.

As with so many other things with YouTube, you'll have to experiment to see what works best for you and your audience. If you're not sure what's working, just ask your viewers! They love sharing their thoughts, especially knowing you'll actually be reading them. They'll be able to provide you with guidance and ideas if you're not sure how you're doing.

Batch Recording: Preventative Medicine for Burnout

There'll be days when you absolutely don't feel like doing a video. But what happens when you've promised videos on Mondays and your eager audience is expecting an upload? Well, you can push through and risk burnout, you could skip a day (way preferable to burnout), or better yet, you could batch record videos. Modern video production is non-linear, giving you the freedom of flexibility in nearly every aspect of the production process. For example, on a day when you *are* feeling motivated to create, why not knock three or four videos out? You don't have to edit them that night or even review them once that red record button turns off. Just tuck them somewhere so that when you're ready to edit, they're right there. You can go as far as batch-producing and uploading videos, and then schedule them weeks in advance using YouTube's Scheduled video option.

Recording

For most videos, this is probably the easiest part of the whole production process. Unless you're going buck wild with multi-camera rigs, ornate livestream productions or producing something resembling *Transformers*, you simply press the record button on your device of choice and go. If you're doing a walk-and-talk or other selfie-focused production, selfie sticks can help prevent video shake and arm fatigue. They can look pretty silly, but they do a great job of upping production values. Going in front of a camera, even doing a screencast, can be nerve wracking. After hundreds of videos, I still get nervous and sometimes have to say the same line ten to fifteen times over. Fortunately, our special friend the video editor can save the day.

Editing

Editing is where the magic happens. The editing process is where you take a piece of carbon and pressure-blast it into a diamond, transforming a rambling 30-minute diatribe into a tightly-edited 8-minute piece of video art. That's no small task.

When you get to know your video editor, it'll be your best friend and secret weapon as a YouTuber. Knowing when and how to use certain functions, features, and effects is what separates the best YouTubers from the rest of the heap, whether those people have 500 subscribers or 5 million.

For example, most editors have a blade function. This is going to be the most important function in the entire editor, as it lets you slice pieces of your video out that aren't important to the topic. I use the blade **religiously** on videos that aren't scripted, but sometimes even scripted videos get cut because there's a piece of unnecessary fluff.

"Why this obsession with editing, cutting, and trashing video clips?" you may be asking. "Don't you get better engagement rates with longer videos because people are staying longer?"

Here's the thing: people have really short attention spans. Like, *really* really short. The average watch time on my hundreds of videos is consistently around 3 minutes. Many other YouTubers report this same kind of dismal number. Does that mean the video sucks? Not necessarily. It's that whole attention span thing. That said, a lot of people *do* stick around for the entire video so it's critical that you edit your video in a way that respects your viewers' time without rushing through it or cutting corners.

I try to keep my current videos between 6 and 10 minutes. It's a good length of time that lets me cover my topics, respects my audience's time, and keeps them coming back for more. There's a **lot** of editing that takes place with my videos. Many times the original video files are 20 or 30 minutes long! I make a lot of mistakes, get sidetracked a lot, need to sip my coffee, and get interrupted by my cat Celina quite often (she claims she's just trying to help).

It might feel weird for you as you put in all that video production effort only to come out with a six minute video, but it's just a reality of the editing process. In the long run, editing your videos tightly will pay off for you and keep your viewers coming back for more.

If you produce a video that delivers your message, without cutting corners,

while respecting peoples' time – you're already 90% there.

If you're worried about editing and getting people to stick around, one hack to improving audience retention and watch times is to do a lot of longer livestreams (like 30 minutes to an hour) since more people tend to stick around for those.

Conversely, pre-recorded videos that are 20 to 30 minutes long – covering a topic that could be produced in 10 minutes or less – is a recipe for disaster. For one, most people aren't coming to YouTube for longer-form material. Secondly, it does a nasty thing to your engagement rate since people are only staying 2 or 3 minutes for a half-hour video. The other benefit of livestreams is that you can't do any editing or other major post-production on those, so they're relatively quick to produce.

Exporting for YouTube

Many video editing apps have an export setting built specifically for YouTube. The bitrate, audio and video codecs, and other technical details are built-in to these presets so it's essentially one-click publishing. For example, Premiere Pro has a YouTube 1080 HD preset that lets you export in high definition. They even have a fancy 2160p 4K preset.

If your editing program doesn't have a custom preset for YouTube, you can create one. But because all editors are different, listing all the possible export settings and variations here would be a book in itself. A simple search of your video editor plus "export for YouTube" (i.e. *final cut pro export for youtube*) should do the trick.

Publishing

OK, so now your video is exported, but how do you get it from Point A (your local machine) to Point B (the YouTube servers)? Fortunately YouTube makes the process easy. Just navigate to

YouTube, sign in, and in the upper right corner is a video camera icon with a plus sign in the middle. Click it, click *Upload video*, and then you simply select the video you want to publish. This is also where you'll add your video title, thumbnail, description, tags, and other video extras like end screens (linking to other videos and playlists of yours). Once the video is uploaded and processed, you have a few options for sharing it with the world. You can immediately publish it, you can schedule it for a future time and/or date, or you can schedule a Premiere.

Premieres let your subscribers know that you're about to publish a video. They're able to save it, get notified by YouTube when it's premiering and watch it along with you. You also get the chat function added to your video premieres, creating a built-in real-time audience engagement tool. Premieres are especially well-suited for longer videos –– you can interact with people and keep them engaged in the chat when they may have normally clicked another video. This not only creates a fun environment for your subscribers but it also boosts that all-important metric: watch time. This ultimately tells the YouTube algorithm that your video is one that people care about and ideally gets you featured in more recommended video slots.

Browser Extensions: Tools for Bigger & Better Videos

There are a number of valuable browser extensions you can start using right away to help with the planning and execution of your video ideas.

Keywords Everywhere

The first is Keywords Everywhere. This extension is available for Firefox and Chrome. If you're wondering how popular one of your video ideas is, or you're looking for a better way to title your video, or you're looking for some similar keywords other people are searching, or you're comparing ad rates for certain keywords, start using Keywords Everywhere.

This extension is indispensable for research purposes and when used appropriately it can help you get consistently more views and higher engagement rates. It's super easy to use: after installation, go to Google and type in a keyword or keyphrase. Right beneath the Google Search bar you will see the search volume (how many people search the term per month) along with it's CPC (cost per click). So not only are you seeing how popular a term is, you're also seeing how much that term is worth to advertisers. The CPC is relevant because the higher the CPC, the higher your earnings are if the advertiser's ad plays on one of your videos.

For example, let's say you have a bubblegum review channel. If the term "Worst Bubblegum 2019" has a search volume of 12,000 and a CPC of $1.20, and the term "Best Bubblegum of 2019" has a similar search volume but a CPC of $12.20, it may benefit you financially to do a video on the best bubblegum of 2019 rather than the worst. There is no guarantee that you'll get matched with an advertiser related to best bubblegum of 2019, but by optimizing your video (discussed in the next chapter) you will exponentially increase your chances of this fruitful match.

Note: You can also use this extension right on the YouTube search bar, but its functionality is limited in that it doesn't show you similar terms. Since YouTube is owned by Google, the search volume and CPC on YouTube mirrors the results you would find using Google.com.

Tags for YouTube

This release is also available for both Chrome and Firefox. Tags for YouTube does exactly what it says: it shows you the tags people added to their videos. Simply install the extension and in the comment box area next to the category and licensing info, the tags pop up. This dead-simple extension is perfect for researching your competition and taking notes on what successful YouTubers in your niche are using for tags.

vidIQ

vidIQ is another good extension, but as of publication it's only available for Chrome. This is a tier-based extension and the basic plan is free (the paid tiers may be worth the investment once you start building a subscriber base – there are lots of features). vidIQ has a crazy amount of useful information available on the free tier -- it's kind of a like an all-in-one channel audit for you or your competitor's videos. What is the like-to-dislike ratio on a video? How many comments contain questions or have replies? How many external webpages are linking to your video? The answer to these questions and dozens of others are available to you for free with vidIQ.

Summary

In this chapter you learned about your YouTube workflow and how each component helps you make better videos. From setting up a video publishing schedule to batch recording; from gathering video topics and researching their viability to religiously using the blade tool in your video editor for tightly-edited engaging videos; all the way to discovering useful browser extensions, setting up your workflow is a cornerstone of your sustained success as a small YouTuber.

Next up, we're going to go beyond the basics of what you just learned and talk about going *beyond* the video.

YOUTUBE 2.0: CONTENT CREATION

Going Beyond the Video

I always thought the term "content creator" was pretty clinical. It makes me think of cold patties of content being flipped by transactional middlemen, we YouTubers a mere cog in the machine yet a barrier to what the consumer wants: *content*. But despite my disdain for the term, it does a better job at explaining what we do compared to the term *video producer* or even *YouTuber*. After all, producing the video is only **part** of what we do. Engaging with our audience, writing accompanying blog posts, creating eye-catching thumbnails, doing expansive keyword research and optimizing our titles are a handful of other things we're responsible for once we enter the world of YouTube.

In this chapter, we're going to focus on the things that support the video; things that transform you from a humble video maker to a three-dimensional content creator. You're going to work on building components that help form the "package deal." As a result, you'll gain more subscribers while keeping the ones you have entertained, satisfied, and coming back for more.

These components include:

- A snappy title
- An attention-grabbing thumbnail
- A video description optimized for SEO
- A pinned comment
- Audience engagement

Extras we'll also cover:

- An accompanying blog post
- Social media sharing

Let's kick it off with one of *the* most important components on any YouTube channel: the title.

The Title: A Vehicle for Clicking

Fun fact: The title and the thumbnail are the reasons people click on your video.

One more time, with gusto: *The title and the thumbnail are the reasons people click on your video.*

Let that sink in for a minute! We often spend lots of time editing our videos to perfection—and you *do* have a spiffy-looking production when you're done, but that's not what makes people click on your video. The video is what makes people **stay** for your video, but what gets them in the door?

Your title and your thumbnail.

Naturally, you want the title and thumbnail to be as enticing as possible: something that succinctly sums up your video yet grabs the attention of both diehard and casual viewers alike.

Early on, I was careless with titles. I was self-indulgent and often embraced my whimsical nature over everything else. Having no technique for naming my videos, there was both a lack of consistency and an abundance of fluff words. Unsurprisingly, not a lot of people tuned in. Some early examples of my dead-on-arrival titles:

BITCOIN review: My first experience, I got paid. (I think)

Codingphase -- reviewing the good, the bad, & the ugly!!

I *just* experienced a technical phone interview (fullstack web development)

PHP, a working woman's programming language

Some of these are way too wordy and others give little to no indication of what the heck I'm talking about. For example, *PHP, a working woman's programming language?*

What does that even mean?

That video clocks in at just over three minutes (too short!) and I'm basically showcasing a behind-the-scenes look at one of my PHP projects involving a platform called WeBid, while giving some commentary on why I think PHP is great.

Now, here are some examples of how I could optimize that title for both humans and SEO:

A few things I love about PHP || New PHP Project Idea

What I love about PHP in 3 minutes || PHP Project Idea (WeBid)

Web Developer Discovers PHP || New PHP Project Idea (WeBid)

Any of these three titles is light-years ahead of my original title. They're descriptive, they hit on my keyphrase ("PHP project idea"), and they're accurate without being a snooze. From a viewer standpoint, aren't those so much better than *PHP, a working woman's programming language?*

By now, you might be wondering how to take your own videos and video ideas and extract a good title. There's no standardized way of doing it, but here's my four-step formula for creating titles:

1. State subject of video, trying to match the keyword/keyphrase as closely as possible.

2. Add a statement that sums up the "higher idea" of the video.
    -Or rephrases the subject.
    -Or expands with some teaser details.
    -Or uses a keyword/keyphrase.

3. Go back, shorten, simplify.

4. Go back and optimize for target keyword/keyphrase.

Here are some examples of "final draft" titles:

The new Captain Marvel website is a TRAINWRECK || 90s website design

Web Developer Roadmap 2019 || The guide to becoming a dev

CodingPhase.com review (first look) || online code school

Native image lazy-loading is coming to the web! || Faster Frontend Web Development

Should she go to this bootcamp? || DigitalCrafts Coding Bootcamp

Not all of my videos follow this formula. Sometimes I'll pique viewer interest simply by asking a question, or taking the less-is-more approach depending on the topic:

Google is releasing a game console

Is jQuery dead in 2019? || 150 developers respond!

Is Ruby worth learning in 2019? || 200+ developers respond!

HTML & CSS demo for frustrated newbies

If monkeys can code, why do we?

What is the future of React and Vue?

See how succinct most of these titles are?

But sometimes titles *need* to be long – for example, maybe a title of a book is lengthy – but don't fill up the title box just because you can. Your potential viewers need to be able to quickly glance at a title, then quickly glance at a thumbnail (or vice-versa) and determine whether or not your video is worth watching. You don't want to hinder that process with long titles or empty words.

Here are some examples of bloated titles, adapted from some of the examples above:

What do you think the future of React and Vue is for web development?

Google announced it'll be releasing a game console soon

Here's the web developer roadmap that helps your coding journey!!

CodingPhase.com code school first look online review, what was it like?

Avoid wordiness, however tempting: it's those short, succinct titles make people click on videos. When it's not possible to be short, be succinct.

The thumbnail: The *other* vehicle for clicking

The thumbnail is the other thing people use to gauge their interest in a video. Creating a compelling thumbnail is also important when you're making videos with topics that are commonly covered, or at least covered by more than just you. It makes you stand out and get clicks.

So what makes a good thumbnail?

Simply stated, a good thumbnail is an image that captures the attention of your audience without misleading them.

A thumbnail that almost always gets peoples' attention is when it appears to be "responding" to the title. For example, if the title is "HTML is dead? || 500 developers share their thoughts!" the thumbnail could be of a person giving a perplexed look with a furrowed brow –– HTML isn't dying anytime soon. I've used emojis instead of people (the Thinking Face Emoji is a particular favorite) with great results.

While it can be a hard technique to execute and there are certain titles and topics where it's not possible, think about where you can really fuse the title with the thumbnail. The combination will give your videos a new depth and sense of liveliness rather than just a photo with text on it.

Let's take a look at a few thumbnails and titles that work well together.

Title: *New JUNIOR WEB DEVELOPER Job Board || Developer Needs Feedback! || gojuniors.co*

Cats have very little to do with tech jobs, but this thumbnail plays off the title nicely. The cat looks on, pondering the possibilities of this new job board for junior web developers. And because the developer of the site needs feedback, it appears as if the cat is *extra*-pondering this new addition to the web.

Notice how the concept of the video is typed in the thumbnail with bright colors and a bigger-sized font – another good attention-grabbing technique. But mind the font's readability: most times I'll put a heavy stroke (outline) on my text so it's easier for people to see from afar.

Finally, a screenshot from the actual job board serves as a background for the image, positioned so that three web development buzzwords (JavaScript, Angular, TypeScript) are shown, underscoring the tech theme and reminding people it's not just about the cat.

Here's another one:

Title: WINDOWS vs MAC vs LINUX || Best OS for web development 2019

For this one I created a gradient to complement the colors of the Apple and Windows logos, while giving the Linux penguin some soul in his eyes. Vibrant and eye-catching, the additional googly-eyes on the apple give this thumbnail a new sense of life, however wacky. Operating system videos have a tendency to be very serious and buttoned up, so this playful style on this one is another way for me to grab peoples' attention.

A lot of the gurus will tell you to be consistent with your thumbnails (same fonts, colors, etc.) as well as to add your branding (like your logo placed on the artwork). You can go for that, but honestly, I like to change it up as a small YouTuber. Once I get a bigger audience I might take their advice, but I **always** create the thumbnail to fit the optimized video title.

For example, is the title aggressive ("JavaScript DOMINATES programming in 2019")? In that case, I'll use an aggressive/ragged font in the thumbnail with bold colors and an angular design. Is it a feel-good story? That calls for soft colors and smoother text on my part. Again, it's up to you if you want to go guru-mode, but I really haven't had particular success using their cookie-cutter formula.

Help, I Stink at Design

If you weren't blessed with a knack for Photoshop, no worries. While I do recommend learning the basics of graphic design, in the meantime you could either hire somebody to make your thumbnails for you or use a free photo editing site that has a library of picture editor effects and photo filters. One of my favorites is photofunia.com. They also have a lot of cool advanced text-based presets (like this cool old-school one: https://photofunia.com/effects/retro-wave). If that site isn't your cup of tea, just Google "free photo filter app online" or "free photo editing app online."

Keep practicing and you'll get better at thumbnail design. I've designed hundreds over my channel's history and pick up new techniques and ideas all the time.

Writing a Video Description

Taking the time to write a thorough video description is important for a few reasons.

Firstly, when people are searching video topics, they're able to see the first few lines of that description, letting them assess whether or not your video is what they're looking for.

Secondly and perhaps more importantly, everything you write can be used for SEO purposes. For example, if you're trying to rank for the keyphrase "sea bass fishing tutorial," search engines like Google are more likely to recommend the video to people when you use that phrase a few times throughout your description.

You don't have to go hog wild with descriptions, but you should be writing at least a paragraph (5-8 sentences) that naturally repeats your keyword or keyphrase. Think about what a huge competitive advantage this gives you compared to other YouTubers. Most don't bother writing anything, or they fill the box with links and promos used in all their other videos. Or, when they do write descriptions, they're one or two sentences only. There's lots of opportunity here for you!

Need some examples? Here are a few from some of my videos.

Example 1.

Welcome to Episode 2 of the Freelance Newbie podcast! In this podcast we're talking all about freelancing.

If you've got tech skills, you've got a way to make money.

It doesn't matter if you've just started learning HTML & CSS or you're a senior developer at a large company — the things we talk about apply to all abilities. Whether you're wondering where to start, how to engage with people so they want to do business with you, or just want to get some ideas for that sweet, sweet cash, Freelance Newbie is a podcast that is all about real-world scenarios.

No FizzBuzz challenges here! In this episode of Freelance Newbie we're taking a look at four major ways you can start earning some major money as a developer.

The Freelance Newbie podcast is made possible by RTC Patreons! Please consider joining a great group of people while helping spread free tech knowledge to the world. If you can't afford it, a Like, Share, or Comment goes a long way too! www.patreon.com/realtoughcandy

Example 2.

What makes you want to walk away from coding?

Well, nearly 400 code newbies recently answered that question, and dozens of people sounded off. From family obligations to imposter syndrome to just too much stuff to learn, in this video these developers are sharing exactly what's getting under their skin.

Stack Overflow's yearly survey consistently reports that the overwhelming majority of developers consider themselves at least partially self-taught.

In other words, most developers who considered themselves self-taught eventually got tech jobs (this is great news). So what exactly is a self-taught developer and why do we have struggles?

A self-taught developer usually doesn't have a college degree in computer science or other tech-related subjects or they don't have a degree at all. These devs have learned to code while working, taking care of their family, along with other life obligations.

The amount of self-determination and focus is massive for self-taught developers, plus time management is another critical factor. As we discuss in this video, it's way too easy to get lost in the rabbit hole of computer science and web development technologies and concepts. There is just so much to learn! Check out today's video and you'll hear dozens of self-taught developer stories where they share their challenges with honesty and insight.

❖ ❖ ❖

Title + Description + Keyphrase = Results

Now let's take it a step further with more context. Note how the target keyphrase shows up in both my titles and descriptions.

Video title: *The Complete Web Developer in 2019: Zero to Mastery by Andrei Neagoie // Udemy course review*
Keyphrase I'm targeting: *complete web developer in 2019*
Video Description:

"The Complete Web Developer in 2019: Zero to Mastery is blowing up in popularity on Udemy.

The title is ambitious, the material is expansive, and the instructor promises real-world skills that will majorly help get you job by the end of the course.

But with the ever-expanding ten dollar zero-to-hero Udemy bootcamps, is this one worth your time and money? Somebody pass me my certificate of near-completion!

Today we're taking a look at The Complete Web Developer in 2019: Zero to Mastery course to see if and how you may be able to benefit from it as an aspiring web developer."

This video currently shows up on the first page of Google Search when people search that keyphrase, and it's the third video that shows up when searched on YouTube. That's awesome, but remember: while the first page is our goal, lots of users *do* go to the second page! So, don't dismiss your efforts if you haven't been rewarded the gold medal in search results yet. For example, despite the video below having some strong and tough competition, it has a few thousand views and counting:

Video title: *Big list of companies HIRING & MENTORING junior developers! // Junior Developer Jobs 2019*
Keyphrase I'm targeting: *junior developer jobs*
Video Description:

"Have you ever submitted a really good cover letter and resume, submitted a really good portfolio to employers and received the dreaded response: *Thanks for your reply but we're looking for somebody with a little more experience?*

Those emails stink.

Well, a developer on Twitter recently did what we were all hoping somebody would do. She reached out to the world and said *Hey, does your company actually support junior developers? Does it offer junior developer jobs? Let me know; I'm making a list.*

Today we're checking out this goldmine of opportunity for junior devs...

The avalanche of junior developer jobs starts now!"

Some YouTube superstar consultants recommend writing no less than 300 words per description – a short blog post, basically, on your video page. I usually don't go that far with mine, but the more you write, the more opportunity you'll have to insert your keyword or keyphrase. Like any written material on the web, make sure the content you write is relevant to the video, accurate, and natural-sounding.

You're also able to add up to three hashtags in your description that will appear right above the video title. Take advantage of this, as well. For example, the above video features the hashtags #udemy, #webdevelopment and #codenewbie.

Strategizing & maximizing with pinned comments

This is an underutilized feature but oh-so-powerful. Each video allows you to "pin" a comment to the top of your comment section. You can either pin somebody else's golden comment or pin your own.

What I'll usually do is add a link or some other bit of helpful information to give more context to my video. This adds value to your audience rather than simply serving as another marketing vehicle.

First, delivering the value:

Thanks for all the great comments in yesterday's video! Still catching up with them! Here's the GitHub repo for companies that hire and mentor junior developers: www.awesomerepo.com

Then, below the fold, I'll deliver the call to action and include links to my courses, books, Patreon page, website, and more.

Marketing experts tell you to provide one solid, simple call to action. I like to give people options. The above example is a soft call to action, simply sharing some options with people to support the channel. I'll also publish these links in my comment box.

Tags

The modest box beneath your video description in the upload area may look innocent enough, but don't bypass the tag area. This is where you tag your video with keywords/keyphrases and is known as meta information. Lots of people have opinions on how many tags to include but I find that being honest and succinct works best. Plus, that takes the guesswork out of tagging so you can focus on more important things in your production process.

I usually use three to five tags, starting with my target keyword/keyphrase and add a few related terms. You can also reference your username or website in your tags if you're trying to rank for your brand name in search results.

Tags for my video on opening a PHP file in your browser (30,000+ views) are simple and succinct: *php, web development, how to code in php, what is php, and how to open php file in browser.*

Joining Your Own Community: Audience Engagement

Have you ever left a comment on a YouTube video and not received a response from the creator? Whether you were expecting one or not, your comments have no doubt gone overlooked by creators. Conversely, have you ever left a comment on a YouTube video and had the creator respond? How did it make you feel?

If you're like a lot of viewers, you probably had a sense of validation or at least enjoyed getting acknowledged. It maybe felt like your voice mattered and that somebody was actually listening. It maybe even felt like somebody cared –– even if you never met them.

Engaging with your audience is one of the best things you can do to attract and keep channel viewers. Because once you start caring, once you start interacting and taking a genuine interest in what people have to say – **they** start caring and interacting. Engaging with your audience not only makes people feel validated and special – it lets you understand them better so you can make better videos. It also increases your trust factor – a powerful thing that can only be earned. And another big benefit? Audience members are great for suggesting new and relevant video topics.

On my channel, I read every comment that comes my way and respond to most of them. Engaging with my audience is a big part of what I do and it's a big part of why a lot of people keep coming back. As a creator, I'm not just *making* a video anymore: I'm *engaging*. Interacting with my audience makes me feel more human...It would be a really one-dimensional experience never interacting with people who enjoy my videos.

Remember, people who make comments are a minority of viewers who went out of their way to engage. Unless they're trolling or otherwise being jerks, show them that they're special and that you care, even if it's just a simple, "Hey Bernard! Thanks for watching. Cheers!" type of response.

And don't forget the "off-YouTube" ways you can also engage with your YouTube audience while strengthening your community ties:

- Chatroom
- Social Media
- Private message/email
- Forum

With the sea of metrics that YouTube provides through its Analytics section, sometimes things can feel impersonal. But remember, behind the numbers are real people with faces, feelings, and ideas. It's true, many people will always be lurkers -- and that's OK. But for those who participate, they are your VIPs and MVPs.

Channel Audit: Pruning the Excess (and Boosting your Profile)

Once you start racking up some videos, it's a good idea to do a channel audit periodically. This is to ensure that your older videos can continue to provide value to your viewers rather than get lumped into the heaping pile of forgotten videos. There are millions of forgotten videos collecting dust on YouTube, neither directly searched for by users nor suggested by the YouTube robots. They simply stop collecting views, crouched and shivering in a small corner of a remote server.

Channel audits can vary in scope, and can be as simple as doing quick spot checks like making sure all your videos titles are spelled correctly, all the way to day-long events where you're reviewing not just the title and thumbnail, but also things like the video description, relevant messaging in the pinned comment, troll or spam/bot comments that may have wiggled their way past your filter, and more.

When you're doing your audit, you may come across videos that you feel just don't represent you, your brand, or your company anymore. It happens to us all: no matter what you change your title to, no matter what image you replace the thumbnail with, the topic is a stinker. You recoil slightly, and quickly and quietly send that video to the trash heap, never to be seen again by you or your viewers.

I've definitely produced my fair share of awful videos and every time I do a channel audit, I do find a few more to either straight-up delete or make private (you just never know when you'll need to break out that review on G.T.'s Cayennade kombucha). It's good to keep your video collection pruned like this, because bad public-facing videos don't reflect good on your metrics like audience retention and watch time –– thus, it's safe to assume YouTube is that much less likely to recommend your channel. It's also a lot easier to navigate your videos that *do* matter when these unintentional horror flicks are out of the way.

Audit checklists

For a simple video audit, ensure that:

- Titles have correct spelling and grammar.
- Titles and thumbnails are optimized.
- Video topic aligns with your current style, brand, and/or business.

For an intermediate audit:

- All of the above
- Video descriptions are written and optimized.
- Pinned comments are completed and optimized.
- Videos have relevant hashtags in description box.
- All links are live and lead to relevant things that will benefit your audience.
- Links are optimized to benefit you as an affiliate rather than the "raw" link that won't give you credit for referral.
- Comment review: remove troll, spam and bot comments.
- Like to Dislike ratio: Remove option to rate video if dis-

likes are too high.
- Out of control comment section: clean up where necessary and change permissions to either "Hold All Comments for Review" or "Hold Potentially Inappropriate Comments for Review." (This is beneath the Advanced Settings tab under "Info & Settings" section of the individual video once you're in editing mode.)

For a full audit:

- All of the above
- Analytics review: What videos are performing the best? Worst? What topics (not just individual videos) drive the most engagement? What is the tone of your comments section? Use this info from your Analytics Panel along with your own observations to guide future videos.

Collaborations: A Surefire Channel Booster

There are probably a few fellow YouTubers in your niche you look up to or at least somewhat enjoy. Why not do a collaboration video with them? Collaborations benefit for you channel in many ways:

- Collaboration videos send viewers from the other person's channel to yours -- many of whom ultimately turn into subscribers.
- Collaborations give you social proof and get subscribers excited ("Oh, Krazy Kathy is doing a collab with Fetchin' Farrah? Rad!")
- Collaborations give you the chance to build a long-term relationship with an important person in your niche.

Collaborations can also be really fun, especially if there's good chemistry between you and your collaborator. It takes courage to cold-email people in your niche, but trust that there are other

YouTubers thinking of doing a collaboration but haven't gotten around to it for whatever reason. They are waiting for your email invitation!

Don't be afraid to reach out to creators who have more subscribers than you. Conversely, be bold in accepting an invite when a YouTuber with more subs wants to create a video with you. I once did a collaboration with a YouTuber who had more than five times my subscriber count and we both had a blast, and I got a *lot* of new, faithful subscribers.

Summary

This chapter covered all the YouTube extras –– the components that frame the video and give it context, all while improving your craft, expanding your audience and increasing audience engagement. From small technical details like hashtags; to more substantial elements like thumbnails and titles; all the way to audience engagement and more; going beyond the video is necessary for every YouTuber regardless of niche.

Now that you've learned about how to get started with producing a channel and making videos, let's move on two Part II: Making Money.

PART II: MAKING MONEY

Welcome to Part II of the book where we explore ways to earn money from your YouTube channel. In the last section, you learned a lot about developing a sustainable channel and now it's time to reap the rewards of your hard work.

Your efforts are not only providing people a quality experience; they're also going to provide you with numerous avenues for making that sweet cash. The seven options we'll discuss are **channel monetization, affiliate marketing, self-produced goods and services, blog, sponsorships, subscriber advertising, and donations.**

As you can see, we go through quite a few options. The key to financial success on YouTube is to **never rely on a single revenue stream.**

Remember, you're using somebody else's platform and earning from somebody else's rules: you're subject to their changes. What happens if a company stops offering an affiliate plan, or YouTube changes its rules for channel monetization again? Or some weird algorithm has deemed your innocent videos on pet cacti inappropriate and thus ineligible for monetization? It's crucial that you diversify your revenue streams because the rules and realities change often.

Before we talk about options and techniques, let's go through the Worst Case Scenario. You should have a plan in place if your channel is terminated, YouTube suddenly goes belly-up, or some other catastrophe hits the YouTube-osphere. Additionally, you should have copies of your videos in case your channel gets zapped. If you don't have your master files or rendered videos on your local machine anymore, there's a really handy service called Google Takeout that lets you download all your YouTube videos.

Now that we have that out of the way, let's talk about the money! First we'll discuss channel monetization.

CHANNEL MONETIZATION

Channel monetization is likely one of the first things people think of when they imagine making money from a YouTube channel. In other words, making money from ads. Whether it's a pre-roll ad (a video ad that plays before the video), a mid-roll ad, an overlay, or something else, every time somebody is exposed to an ad on your channel, you get a cut of the revenue.

Eventually those cuts start adding up. Ever wonder why big-time YouTubers make videos lamenting the latest drama over YouTube algorithms and Adpocalypses? (An Adpocalypse is the term that refers to a mass advertiser boycott on YouTube.)

The reason they're understandably upset is because those millions of views per month are earning them thousands of dollars every couple of weeks. Oftentimes, creators are only relying on their ad money as a source of income, which hurts them even more when the rules change.

Rules and Regulations

It used to be that anybody could apply for monetization on their channel via the YouTube Partner Program and start earning, but that's changed. As of 2019, you need at least 1000 subscribers and

4,000 total watch hours in the last twelve months in order to start earning. You can sign up before that, though, and YouTube will provide an automatic channel review once you reach the threshold.

There are some topics that YouTube will deem too unfriendly for advertisers and there's really no getting around it. This is especially true with politically-based channels and news commentary. Even cursing is often grounds for demonetization (especially the f-bomb). There's no surefire way to guarantee you'll be monetized on videos, but the more PG-rated your videos are, the better chance you have at earning.

To get paid, you will need to sign up for a free AdSense account. This is the advertising arm of YouTube (one of them, anyway), and the one responsible for funneling your ad revenue into your bank account. AdSense is a massive platform, but at the very minimum you'll connect it to your YouTube account and set up your direct deposit info. If you need guidance on this, check out this five-minute walkthrough video.

How Much is a View Worth?

There's no strict formula –– your earnings will vary depending on your niche and your audience location, among other things. Sometimes 1000 views will earn you $2; sometimes 1000 views will earn you $15. As a tech & education channel, my ad rates are higher than many other niches. As of this writing I have about 500,000 views earned over a two-year period: while earnings from those views are nothing to quit my day job over, it's pretty good grocery money.

But no matter what your earnings are per thousand views, the most important thing with monetization is to connect your YouTube account with AdSense, otherwise you won't get paid. Consider setting up AdSense before you even publish your first video so that your very first eligible monetized view is credited to you.

Creators Beware

Channel monetization is the "iffiest" of all the methods for making money on YouTube. You just never know when YouTube will change the rules. However, because it's so easy to get started once you reach the subscriber and watch-time thresholds, it can be an excellent stream of passive monthly income.

AFFILIATE MARKETING

When I first started getting curious about starting a YouTube channel with regularly-scheduled content, I had no idea what affiliate marketing was...But I kept hearing a **lot** about it. I'd watch the "Make a Living on YouTube" videos by Roberto Blake, Tim Schmoyer and the rest of the gang, and they all resounded with the same earnings battlecry: Get started with affiliate marketing.

It just didn't make any sense to me. Marketing? Not my thing. Plus that name just sounded scammy and the process sounded complicated. I was very skeptical.

But in my fog of confusion I ended up signing up as an affiliate with Amazon. I didn't think anything of it, and didn't really use it for much...Until one day I did a video that ended up hitting 20,000 views. It was a review of a learn-to-code platform that I wasn't really impressed with –– so I briefly mentioned an alternative that **was** impressive to me. This alternative was a coding book.

In the pinned comment, I posted an Amazon link for it.

But it was no ordinary link: this one had a special tracking tag in it that attributed every click to me, so that if a person purchased the book I would get a percentage of the sale.

It's really more like affiliate linking rather than affiliate marketing...You don't get paid to talk about the product or service, but you *do* get paid if a person uses your link and buys something.

The key with affiliate marketing is to relate the product to what your video is about. For example, are you doing a favorable review of the Deluxe Limited DVD Edition of *Game of Thrones*? Your audience will probably want to know where they can find it.

Conversely, are you doing an *un*favorable review of that DVD set? Is it the worst thing ever or maybe just a solid "meh?" Just like my online coding platform vs. book approach, you could mention an **alternative** DVD box set you *do* like in the video. Then, link to that item in the pinned comment and video description.

One other cool benefit of affiliate marketing is that even though you're usually linking to one specific product, you'll almost always get credited for everything that person buys on that site.

For example, when a person clicks on your Amazon affiliate link to buy the *Muppet Babies* DVD box set, let's say she also purchases pencils and a Himalayan salt lamp during that same session. Once those items ship, you receive a commission for the DVD box set, the pencils and the salt lamp.

The Process

Some affiliate sites have you go through an application process, which is somewhat obnoxious because the standards are inconsistent. They have you fill out things like your niche, your platforms, your viewership and so on. One week it's "Sorry, not approved" and the next it's "Oh hey, welcome aboard!"

Don't get bummed out if a platform declines your app – just try again sometime later. I got declined from one really fruitful affiliate marketing platform, resubmitted my application a few days later and got accepted immediately, so it's definitely worth trying until you get approval.

Some affiliate sites payout biweekly, some every month, some quarterly. Many also require you to reach a certain sales threshold before they payout. For example, if their threshold is $50 a month but you only earned $40 in commissions that month, you won't get paid that month: that amount will carry over into the next month and continue to carry over until you hit the threshold.

Amazon is the obvious affiliate marketing site to use since it has so much stuff. But there's a lot of stuff it *doesn't* have plus the cookie only lasts 24 hours with a few exceptions. So whatever your niche is, spend some quality time with Google to see what affiliate programs are out there for your specialty. You can start this process even before you make your first video and you'll be prepared to drop the link once you get rolling with video publishing.

Summary

In summary, affiliate marketing isn't as scary or massive as it sounds. Simply stated, you share a link with people and they can click on it. Your unique ID is placed in the link, and every click and subsequent sale is attributed to you. The length of the cookie varies. For each sale completed when your cookie is valid, you receive a commission.

SELF-PRODUCED GOODS AND SERVICES

Another significant revenue stream for tiny YouTubers is self-produced goods and services. That is, instead of promoting, linking, and otherwise selling others' stuff, you sell your own. This has numerous benefits but one of the biggest is that your cut of the profits is a lot larger compared to when you sell on behalf of others. Not only are you able to sell directly to your customers and keep most (or all) of the profits: **others** are now able to sell your goods and services. Offer something that people can get excited about and it can change everything.

It doesn't matter what niche you choose or your education level: there is a product or service you can develop that people both want and need.

Cashing in on Courses

One popular offering is courses. Whether you're a fashionista, RV enthusiast, record collector, cat lady, or anything else, your knowledge and experience is *worth something*.

People use YouTube for entertainment but also for education. There is a significant chunk of your audience that wants to get educated in your niche.

To illustrate: My first course was inspired by my fruitful comment sections. Countless people would leave questions like:

"What projects do I put in my web development portfolio?"

"When should I apply for a job?"

"Should I put a TODO app in my portfolio?"

And many more that centered around getting a job in web development. I sensed a pattern, so after doing some research, I took the plunge and designed my first course, titled simply *How to Get a Job in Web Development.* Taking my knowledge and insight from my own experiences as a developer, I extracted the essence of what aspiring employees need to know and delivered a top-rated course to an eager audience base. And you can do the *exact* same thing.

I decided to deploy the site on Udemy (an online learning platform) and my website. With a runtime of about ninety minutes, it's one of the only courses of its kind of Udemy, which was an important factor when I chose that topic. There are a **lot** of long-established, popular developer educators on Udemy and there was no way I could compete with instructors who had hundreds of thousands of current students. I picked a topic that people were asking for but one that also had little competition.

There's no shame in mentioning that you have a YouTube channel somewhere in your course and in your instructor bio. In fact, many students love this. The cool thing is that as my subscriber base on YouTube grows, so do my numbers on Udemy –– and as my Udemy numbers grow, so does my subscriber base on YouTube! Keep this in mind when selecting topics to teach. If it's a popular topic but has had heavy play by popular instructors in your niche, it's going to be tough going. Better to pick the low-hanging fruit and pursue a topic that your audience is interested in but hasn't been tackled yet. Why not corner the market? It's also a great way to differentiate yourself when working on marketing materials. For example: "Channel XYZ: The only channel to have released a Competitive Cat Combing course – a national best seller!"

As an instructor, you don't have to use Udemy but it's one of the most popular and easiest platforms to deploy on. If you plan on regularly releasing courses, you can also start your own subscription-based platform using the help of platforms like Thinkific or Teachable.

Producing courses can be lucrative but it demands a lot of technical attention. You'll need to educate yourself or find a mentor to walk you through the ropes of creating a professional-grade course. Unlike YouTube where the standards are lower, a paid course has minimum expectations such as consistent audio levels, high-quality video, minimal verbal pauses, etc. Mic quality, vocal control, levels, and other audio concerns are of utmost importance, as is recording quality, smooth editing, and other production values.

One of the best educations you can get is by mimicking the best in the business:

How are the top educators in your niche editing and recording?

How long are the courses and what is the delivery and pace like?

Are they using slides, doing screencasts?

Take notes, grab influence where you can, and practice, practice, practice in your video editor. There are lots of free technical how-tos on YouTube if you get stuck and Udemy also has some courses to get you up to speed with the basics. It may seem daunting at first but once you learn these production skills, you can use them over and over to create multiple income streams just from your various courses.

Beyond Courses

Aside from educational courses, there are many other ways you can make money with self-produced goods and services:

- Books
- Apps
- Clothing items and accessories
- Inventions and gadgets specific to your niche
- Channel Swag like stickers and promo items
- Online services like website building, SEO, blogging
- Consulting/Coaching

And anything else you can think of, really.

The only rule is that in order to gain traction on your channel, **your goods and services must somehow relate to your channel.** If you have a dog enthusiast channel and your products and services involve bingo daubers, not many people in your audience are going to care if you promote your daubers, offer consultations on the best dauber for your clients, or produce a course on the best bingo daubing techniques.

But if you have a dog enthusiast channel and you produce custom dog leashes, *now* people are going to perk up. Conversely, if you have a product or service developed *before* you start you channel, you could consider starting a channel that complements it.

Summary

Self-produced goods and services are a lucrative and sustainable way to make money on YouTube. Unlike ad revenue, you control your pricing and there's no ad blocker for when you discuss your products and services in a video. There are **huge** earning opportunities with self-produced goods and services as a tiny YouTuber since you keep most, if not all of the generated revenue.

BLOG

Your blog can not only drive traffic to your YouTube channel -- you can send your YouTube people to your blog.

With the explosion of online visual entertainment, it may seem counterintuitive to build a site that caters to the written word. But believe it or not, many of us love to read! What's more, the face of blogging has changed considerably over the years. Instead of simply publishing paragraphs with a few pictures scattered about, we're now able to make the experience interactive with videos, comment sections, polls, social sharing buttons, live chat, and so much more.

I always thought "blog" was such an unattractive word for such a rich medium. You can put almost anything in a blog post, and style it completely to fit your personality along with your goals as an entrepreneur, writer, and YouTuber. Blogging is kind of a Web 1.0 technology, but as long as humans are interested in other humans we'll continue to read about each other.

Starting a blog is so easy these days that it's almost always worth the investment as a YouTuber. WordPress is the most popular option, but use what you enjoy. You might even consider something like Shopify if you plan on going heavy with ecommerce.

Wait…This is a book about YouTube…What's the connection with a blog?

Having a blog means you can keep your subscribers in your ecosystem without directing them to a third-party site or app. When you have a blog, you can link to it in your videos both visually (like a slide or endscreen) and aurally ("Big Bad Bobby from BigBadBobby.com back on camera for another video!"), as well as in your video description and your pinned comment. You can even make dedicated videos about your blog if they're compelling enough.

You'll want your blog to contain content that caters to your YouTube audience. For example, if you have an RV channel, the blog should pertain to RVing. When you blog, you can also link to your goods and services section of your website…Which is one more reason to start a blog: the ecommerce opportunities are massive and you get to keep all the revenue minus the payment processor fees.

As another example, when I sell an ebook on Amazon that's priced over $9.99, they take 70% of my sales. That's a big chunk! But when I sell it on my website, I keep over $9 of the $9.99 on that same ebook. Your blog serves as an information center, a direct sales page, a contact hub, and so much more.

My own blog is a section on my website RealToughCandy.com. The site's main focus is ecommerce where I sell my books, videos, and other digital products. My blog complements the topics I discuss on my YouTube channel and will often feature the videos themselves at the top of the blog pages. That way, those coming from Google or another search engine can see right away that I'm on YouTube. This opens my channel up to a new funnel of subscribers. Those who come from YouTube can scroll right past it and pick up some additional information on the topic while having a chance to snag one of my books or other digital products.

Quick but important side note: You can also earn revenue on your site through advertising (i.e embedding ads somewhere on the site using AdSense). If you're using WordPress there are numerous online tutorials along with ample plugins to make the process easier.

Summary

Whether you stick with just a blog or decide on a fully-featured site with a blog section, having a blog has numerous benefits. From selling your own goods and services (and finally being able to keep most of the revenue!), to promoting your videos within a blog post, to funneling your Google traffic to your YouTube channel, these benefits all have monetary values. The startup costs for the typical blog are dirt cheap and this inexpensive investment almost always pays off in the long run.

SPONSORSHIPS

While the idea of a big-name company backing your channel may seem impossible right now, there's a lot more behind the velvety YouTube sponsorship curtain than meets the eye.

Firstly, it's not just the big names that sponsor videos — small businesses, startups, freelancers, "solopreneurs" (one-person business endeavors) and many others all need to get their name out there and do regularly pay for screen time.

Secondly, even if you "only" have a few hundred views per video, that's a lot more than many other marketing avenues. For example, even small-town newspapers charge hundreds of dollars for a printed ad buried inside the paper. How many people are actually reading that? YouTube advertising has countless improvements over many advertising systems that are notorious for being too basic and inefficient.

But here's the catch: instead of the business owners flocking to you, you have to flock to *them*. As a small YouTuber, not only is it hard for the right people to easily find you, many others have simply never even thought of advertising on the platform. The burden is on you to knock on the digital doors. Fortunately, once you have a few videos on your channel you already have some clout when it comes to your pitch.

Before my channel was focused on tech, I had produced several videos where my cat reviewed cat treats. They were cheap little cheesy vids of me ripping open a fresh pack of salmon-mackerel-turkey-whatever treats, setting them on the linoleum floor, and seeing how my cat Celina responded to them. The videos didn't get all that much traffic -- less than 100 views each -- but if it's one thing about cats, they don't lie.

There was one treat in particular where Celina went hog wild, cutely looking at the camera for more once she had demolished the first batch. You don't get a better endorsement of a product than that! A few weeks after posting it, I found the company that produced the treats and sent them the video. Before I could even ask them for anything, the person behind their social media account had arranged for $50 in freebies.

You don't have to be a crazy cat lady to get sponsors -- think about smaller businesses out there that can benefit from exposure on your channel. They are out there.

Working the Local Circuit: A Strategy That Works

Remember that most businesses that get an unsolicited offer are going to send your email straight to trash; unfortunately, as great as you envision your sponsorship, these companies will usually consider your pitch spam. So, instead of sending offers to strangers as a YouTube newbie, we going to *work the local circuit*.

Always start with the low-hanging fruit when seeking sponsors. You can get a lot of business going when you build trust in your local area. (I talk about this topic at length in my other book, *Freelance Newbie*.) Essentially, people want to trust you before they fork over their cash. Fair enough, right? So do take special note when you're out and about with your life activities, focusing on places where you've already built relationships. Could your hair stylist, organization you're a part of, community sports team, corner store where you buy Powerball tickets, or even next-door neighbor benefit from a sponsorship on your channel?

You'd be surprised how many people have something to advertise but end up keeping a low profile. Sometimes the idea doesn't even occur to them until you bring it up: it doesn't hurt to ask, and the worst they can say is no. And when you have a trust factor, however basic it may appear, people are more open to your ideas.

Going digital

You should also comb your online connections you've made over the years. Does anybody in your chat groups or other online social circle need advertising for their company or brand? Just like with the local circuit, it doesn't hurt to ask and the worse they can say no. The approach will probably be via email, and so you can open it up with something really simple and honest. For example, if you're part of an online art community and you've known Tom for a while, you could write something like:

Hey Tom,

How's it going? So I started a new YouTube channel on watercolor painting tutorials (!!). The response has been pretty awesome, 300 subscribers already just from a tutorial I did on color mixing.

Anyway, I've been thinking of you since I know you mentioned you've been developing some brushes. A few people have left comments on how they're looking for better brushes and you immediately came to mind. Would you be interested in talking more about a sponsorship for the channel? If not, no worries –– like I said you just came to mind and I think it would be a great way to get your product out there to a new market. Take care, talk soon! -Stef

Notice how this proposal is informal and low-pressure. While your tone and writing style is going to be different than Stef's, you never want to jeopardize a good relationship by acting pushy or desperate. At the same time, you want the deal to go through, so stay on-topic and focus on the collaboration, telling them how it will benefit them. In this case, Tom will be afforded a bigger audience to sell more paintbrushes.

Movin' On Up: Sponsorship Platforms

Once you reach certain subscriber thresholds, more and more companies start taking notice. Our jobs get easier, we get paid more, and the hustle gets just a tiny bit less strenuous. And one big benefit is that once you reach 5,000 subscribers, there's a platform that makes it easy for advertisers and content creators to connect: FameBit. Once you reach 10,000 subs, your options open up even more with Grapevine.

FameBit

For channels with 5,000 or more subscribers, FameBit acts as a matchmaker for you and advertisers. You sign up, sync your account and can start searching for opportunities based on niche. For example, there are categories for tech, gaming, health and fitness, pets, and a few others. After you find an opportunity that seems to fit, you send a proposal. Why would you be a good fit? How is the company going to benefit? You don't want to drone on in the proposal, but you also don't want to be insensitive with your wording. If you really want to go to the front of the line (or at least get closer to it), tell them what you like about their product or service and how it's helped *you*. Companies want people who are enthusiastic about their offerings, not simply fleshy drones who plug a product. Check out the sample proposal in Appendix B for further guidance.

The big downside to FameBit is that most advertisers are looking for big metrics along with really obvious topics. You may find yourself sending proposal after proposal only to hear crickets after you hit the *Submit Proposal* button. For example, since my niche is very specific with web and software development, there aren't a lot of advertisers on this platform willing to work with that, even in the tech category.

Additionally, compared to other tech channels, my subscriber count is low. Despite this, I do log on to the site a couple times a month just to see what's new -- you just never know what will pop up. If you're in the same boat niche-wise, it doesn't hurt to occasionally prowl the site.

Grapevine

For channels with 10,0000 or more subscribers, Grapevine is also an option. Just like with FameBit, it serves as a matchmaker between the two parties but offers a tad more exclusive feel.

Other Platforms

Other sponsorship matchmaking sites pop up regularly, but tread lightly: some are bogus, other don't work, and others are too new to really know if they're worth your investment. If you find a site other than FameBit and Grapevine, do a Google search to see if it's legit.

Dos and Don'ts for Sponsorship Proposals

Do:

Be enthusiastic and succinct. Everyone's different, and you should never be pressured to be somebody you're not. But writing a stiff, clinical proposal with no enthusiasm in your wording is going to put the reader to sleep, and even worse, most likely put that proposal right in the trashcan. What do you already like or even love about the product or service and the company behind it? Why are you looking forward to working with them? *Tell them.* Tell them like you only have their attention for a few seconds, since that's about how long it takes for them to decide if they want to keep reading or not.

Stay professional and positive. Behind faceless companies are real people, and sometimes those people tick us off. But it's important to stay cool and professional during a not-so-pleasant interaction, especially in the age of social media where another person's or company's comments about you can **destroy** your channel and livelihood. When a sponsor declines your proposal, stay positive, tell them thanks for their consideration, and move on.

Engage business-mode for additional opportunities. Once you've published your sponsored video and got paid, your brain may already be shifting gears to the next task. But sponsorships don't have to be a one-and-done type of deal. If your sponsor liked your video, throw some cool ideas their way for future sponsorships. It doesn't hurt to ask and often they'll be all about it, especially if your video performs well. You could say something like:

Hey Totally_Awesome_Sponsor,

I have a slot open for a video Two_To_Three_Weeks_Down_The_Line.

I have some great ideas for more collaborations with you and know that you do, too. Should I pencil you in?

As you work more with your sponsor, the tone often becomes less stuffy and more fun because you're both making money. This is a great thing!

And now for what **not** to do when pursuing sponsorships.

Don't:

Sell yourself short. If you're asking for $15 and a bunch of samples to do a video review, that could work a few times to build up a portfolio of companies you've worked with. But consistently settling for minimal compensation is only going to set you back in the long run. Think about how much money your mention or dedicated review is going to financially impact the company. Sometimes you're making other entities thousands of dollars with your review! That's certainly worth more than a few bucks and a couple bottles of hairspray.

Act desperate. Desperation is unattractive and ultimately it's selling yourself short. We all want to succeed, and sometimes we do some really weird stuff in order to get ahead.

But it's not going to win proposals. Excessive compliments, begging, and even threats are all no-nos and we definitely don't need this to be a part of our brand's legacy.

Take it personal. You need to have a thick skin in this game. The truth is, most businesses don't want anything to do with us as small YouTubers. Most companies don't care that we exist. Accept this reality and focus on the small percentage of entities that *do* want to work with you, that *can* benefit from you and your YouTube channel. These are the companies who are going to pay your bills and so much more. They exist, they really do; you've just got to connect with them.

Summary

There are many ways to get started with sponsorships. Even better, unlike other money-making vehicles like AdSense ads, sponsorships are based on trust and solid relationships, paving the way for sustainable business relationships throughout your YouTube career and beyond. The next Adpocalypse could hit at any minute, but keep your business relationships healthy and your sponsors will follow you wherever you decide to set up shop.

SUBSCRIBER ADVERTISING

This is a revenue avenue that you never hear about. However, after being active with my channel and community for about a year, I noticed something very interesting about my subscribers.

They were doing a *lot* of cool stuff.

They were making moves! They were starting and building businesses, they were freelancing, they were building their brand, they were trying to get hired...And they were doing a lot of it. I found this out mostly through keeping a keen eye on my comments section while supplementing my information stream with what people were saying in my chatroom along with personal emails people would send.

While it's true that most of your views are coming from people who prefer to stay in the shadows, there's a small but crucial percentage of people who are movers and shakers and don't mind saying so. These are the *exact* people you want to meet.

Gathering and sorting this information, I decided to launch an in-house advertising campaign called the RTC Advertising Network. I designed a simple call to action card and posted it on Twitter and at the end of my videos from time to time, knowing that as long as one or two people paid attention and eventually took the plunge, it would be worth the effort.

I wasn't wrong.

Pictured above is the card I designed to slip into my videos. Sometimes I opened the video with it, other times it was my closing image. One of my subscribers also had his own tech channel and he was trying to boost viewership.

One day he emailed me and asked how much I'd charge to plug his channel.

Since he was part of the community (and also because he was my first customer), I threw out a number: $50 for a 30-second promo at the beginning of an upcoming video. He was so thrilled with my channel, however, that he countered my offer...With a *higher* number.

"That's actually pretty cheap for your channel," he wrote. "I'd like to offer you $100!"

Woah, OK! I happily took my $100 via PayPal, promoted his channel for 30 seconds at the beginning of a video and we both walked away happy. I don't even think this person is active on YouTube anymore, but at the time he was going full-throttle.

When it comes to your own subscriber and peer advertising efforts, it's not just limited to people who have products or services to offer: maybe the person is trying to build their brand by growing their subscriber count or getting their name out there. Maybe they just want to give somebody a shoutout, wish somebody a happy birthday or share a picture of their adorable fur baby.

Make it easy for these people to come forward: in order for the subscriber advertising idea to work, they've got to be exposed to it. Don't be afraid to advertise the advertisement. Why not mention in videos and social media posts that you're doing subscriber and peer advertising?

This type of advertising can be fruitful for you while boosting the community in an authentic way. Believe it or not, many people don't mind ads, and sometimes even enjoy them. Subscriber and peer advertising is a great way to get people involved.

DONATIONS

Some people call it digital panhandling or Internet begging. With these less-than-stellar nicknames, it's no surprise online donations sometimes get a bad rap.

But YouTube is a little different.

Viewers are able to watch our material for free. They don't even need to pay for an Internet connection, as our videos are available just as readily via the library's connection or the local coffeeshop's Wi-Fi. Throw in an ad blocker, and that viewer is enjoying the fruits of our labor for exactly zero dollars, zero cents.

And that's what we love about YouTube, right? When was the last time you felt the urge to call up your local cable provider to hook you up with 500 extra channels when you have five **million** of them on YouTube (which also doesn't require some dude in a jumpsuit flexing cables in your kitchen). YouTube provides a major service to millions of people every second of the day, whether we're needing to watch a tutorial on how to remodel our kitchen or just want to veg out to a mindless junk video. YouTube is there for us free of charge.

That's all to say that most people take free content for granted. However, there is a sliver of your viewership – a *very important sliver* – that believes in what you do. They love your videos, they enjoy your presence, they find value in your work and they want to support it. So what's a creator to do?

One option is to open up avenues for donations. Even if the idea of "Internet begging" turns you off, why should you get in the way of people who want to support your hard work?

In this chapter, we'll cover three major avenues for donations: Patreon, Paypal, and Super Chat.

Patreon

Right now the most popular platform for connecting donors to creators on YouTube is Patreon. Donors (called Patrons) log on to your personal Patreon page to make their pledge. The cool thing about Patreon is that you can offer fun bonuses, perks, and prizes for people depending on how much they donate.

For example, for a $1/month tier, you could offer a shoutout to that person in a video. At the $8/month tier, they get a nifty die-cut sticker, access to your video idea list, and any other rewards on the lower tiers. Depending on how long they've been a Patron, you could also send them a personalized link where they can download your video courses and books as a perk for supporting the channel.

Pros of Patreon? It has the name recognition, it's easy to use, it's another way to share your story with people (Patreon essentially gives you your own landing page), and the perks Patrons receive can be really fun.

Patreon does take a cut of your earnings, but it's similar to what you would find with most other online payment processors.

You can place your donation links in your video description area, as part of a Pinned Comment, and mention them in your video.

PayPal

PayPal works perfectly for one-time donations and/or for donors who don't want to fuss with Patreon. You simply provide a link and they take it from there, entering the amount they want to send. Even better, PayPal donations are instantly yours, unlike Patreon which pays out monthly.

If you don't have a PayPal account, to get started you'll just need an email or mobile number. From there, once you confirm your identity you can add a bank account if you need to transfer funds.

You can make it even easier for people to pay you with PayPal.me. This is a vanity URL service you connect to your PayPal account that's easily mentioned in-video or via the description box or pinned comment.

For example, instead of saying "...You can support the channel via PayPal; my address is QueenAwesomeSauce@gmail.com," you can say, "Support me via a one-time donation by visiting Paypal.me/AwesomeSauce."

Super Chat

If you have at least 1000 subscribers, Super Chats are available to viewers when you do a YouTube livestream. In the chat area, they pledge a donation to you as you're streaming. To see your earnings via Super Chat during your livestreams, navigate to the Creator Studio, then click Community → Super Chat.

The bonus for Super Chat users is that once they donate, their questions or comment gets highlighted, acting as a pinned comment during the stream. It's a great way for subscribers to get their question to the front of line while you make a few bucks from the stream. You'll receive the Super Chat revenue via AdSense.

Patreon, PayPal, and Super Chat are the biggies, but there are many more donation-centric platforms out there, including DonorBox, Kickstarter, and GoFundMe.

CONCLUSION

In this book you learned how to get started as a newcomer to the wild world of YouTube. The platform has changed a lot since it started and every so often it seems like there's yet another algorithm tweak, Adpocalypse, or backlash that threatens to reduce the livelihood of small YouTubers.

Despite these waves of uncertainty, YouTube continues to dominate peoples' lives as a source of continuous entertainment and education, opening up doors to creators who want to share their videos on the 'Tube.

Whether you're planning on doing just a few videos a month, or want to dive right into the daily video grind; whether you want to just make some extra money or make this a full-blown, full-time career, YouTube is the go-to platform to share dynamic, diverse, and exciting video content. There are so many ways to share your story and just as many ways to make money doing it. Hopefully this book gave you some new and valuable ideas to get you started with a successful YouTube channel.

Good luck with your YouTube endeavors, and don't forget to have some fun! -RTC

APPENDIX A:

New YouTuber Questions

I'm shy. Do I really have to be on camera?

The quick answer is no. Yay for many of us, right? But people like seeing other people on camera and that can really help boost your view counts. When they see you, it helps viewers feel a connection -- like they're part of your life and livelihood, even if your channel has nothing to do with your personal life. It's my personal opinion that a channel that doesn't show the creator's face won't perform as well as a channel that *does* show the person. In fact, my videos where I show myself have performed better on average than when I do voiceover videos. But you know what? It's not all that important to me nowadays.

What's more important to me is my sanity, and most days I honestly don't feel like going on camera. Other days -- most days...OK, everyday -- I'm not in the mood for the scrutiny and weirdos. So now almost all of my videos are voiceover (i.e. screencast) only. Most importantly, I still deliver a huge value to my audience. My opening montage also shows a brief video clip of me, helping to establish the voice behind the camera. So if you're shy about putting yourself on camera, don't ever think you can't be a YouTuber because of it. Countless other creators are still producing valuable and popular videos even if they're not going on camera. Focus on producing the value you're delivering to your viewers and you can't go wrong.

These trolls are really starting to get on my nerves. How do I get rid of them? Or better yet, how do I stop them from commenting in the first place?

Trolls are lousy little creatures that try to ruin your day with nasty, lewd, crude, and hey-everyone-look-at-me-I'm-derailing-the-conversation remarks. Fortunately, by taking a proactive approach you can do away with most of them.

First, you should create a list of words you don't want to see on your channel. Just remember that some words you choose may have an innocent context and will also be sucked up by the filter. For example, if you don't want anybody commenting on your hair, but somebody casually mentions the phrase "by a hair," it still goes into the "Held for Review" quarantine area. However, you can approve that type of comment via the link that displays on the individual video or you can access it via Community → Comments → Held for Review in your Creator Studio area.

Once in your Creator Studio, go to Community → Community Settings and then navigate to Blocked Words. Then just type out the words you don't want to see. Right below, there's also an option to block hashtags and URLs, a common spam tactic (but also used a lot by human viewers).

Next, if you have a troll, pervert, weirdo, creep, etc. whom you never want to hear from again, you can ban them.

To do this, start by deleting their comment via the trashcan in the Comments section (Community → Comments in your Creator Studio). Next, click on their username. Then click on their About tab, and beneath it you will see a flag. Once you click the flag, you have a few options. If your troll was really out of line, you can report them. However, if you simply want them out of your life, or at least your YouTube channel, click "Block User." They will no longer be able to leave comments in any of your videos with this account.

I don't want to deal with comments or risk a bad ratio with the thumbs up/thumbs down buttons. Should I disable them?

There may be some times when you want to disable every bit of interaction on some of your videos because of haters and whatever other YouTube bycatch. But this also hurts your quality viewers and subscribers -- the people you care about -- who want to be a part of the channel. Unfortunately, trouble makers always stand out, so sometimes it appears as if they're the only ones participating on your channel. But the truth is, most people watching *aren't* haters and *do* want to at least have the **option** of sharing their thoughts.

If your video is attracting a lot of hate or dislikes/disapproval from various users, it may be best to just take the video down altogether; a disabled comment section and Like/Dislike buttons can really hurt business.

As a YouTuber who also spends time on YouTube watching videos, I tend to not subscribe to channels where my thoughts via the comment section aren't welcome. I can live without a like/disklike button, but I at least want the option of sharing what I think of the video.

Disabling a comment section is kind of like the digital version of a Walmart greeter saying: "Welcome to Walmart. Get Your s*** and get out." On the other hand, sometimes I'll disable Likes and Dislikes once one of my videos hits a big number (non-subscribers will always be more critical of your material), and the like-to-dislike ratios get a little skewed; and I'll also set hot videos to "Hold All Comments for Review" to weed out trolls before they make the main video page.

I see a lot of YouTubers doing giveaways. Should I give stuff away, too?

When I first started my channel, I was very impatient: I wanted the subscribers to flock to it, but it wasn't happening! RealTough-

Candy had about 300 subscribers when I did my first giveaway, a popular learn-to-code book. All viewers had to do was be subscribed to the channel and leave a comment. A few weeks later, I'd pull a name out of a hat and send the book to the winner.

The contest came and went, I heard from a few people I'd never heard from, and life went on.

Not a very exciting story, huh?

Contests are a waste of time for small channels if your purpose is to drum up hype and engagement beyond one video. Sure, you'll get a few new people chiming in because they're hoping to win – but rather than spend $10-40 on a prize, you could be investing that money in other things for your channel, like putting it towards a nicer mic, better camera, or higher-quality cables.

Ultimately, giveaways like this are unsustainable if you're goal is to gain engaged subscribers. For channel growth, it's better to focus on developing what subscribers really came for – you and your awesome videos. Think about it this way: have you ever seen a comment on any YouTube video asking for the creator to do a giveaway? Conversely, you've probably seen many comments requesting that the creator address a certain topic or imploring the creator to improve their mic and camera quality.

But let's say you're not in it for the self-promotion. If you're just trying to have fun and meet a few people from your subscriber base, then contests and giveaways can be perfect for that. It's a great way to meet the people who watch your videos and it's always nice hearing from new people. Some may not have much to add when it comes to your video review of a reproduction leg lamp from *A Christmas Story*, but give one of those things away and lots of eyes and ears perk up.

What's this Sub-4-Sub thing I keep hearing about?

Sub for sub is when a person subscribes to your channel if you subscribe to theirs. You see it a lot in the comment sections of

SEO and be-a-better-YouTuber videos. It's intended to pump up your numbers while returning the favor to a stranger. However tempting (who doesn't like higher subscriber numbers?), avoid sub for sub schemes. They really hurt your metrics – your sub-for-sub trader isn't going to watch your videos – and as a YouTuber who's in it for the long haul, you don't need sub for sub helping prop up your channel. Why settle for a scam when you've got the talent and knowledge to earn real subscribers? Instead of sub for sub, work on growing an authentic subscriber base using the techniques discussed in this book and you will have *way* better numbers than ever possible with sub for sub stuff.

Is there a way to trigger the algorithm? Video gurus are always mentioning this.

Triggering the YouTube algorithm is a topic that always gets peoples' attention, but the truth is, the sacred YouTube algorithm is proprietary. That is to say, nobody except its developers, and probably a few lucky others who are sworn to secrecy, know what it is.

It's a secret.

It's also a mind-boggling large mathematical formula, and anybody claiming to know how it works should be taken with a very large grain, perhaps an iceberg, of salt. Most YouTubers whose videos have gone viral will affirm that they had no idea it was going to blow up like it did. Your best bet is simply to make videos to the best of your abilities, focusing your efforts on high-quality, high-value content that your audience loves.

APPENDIX B:

Sample Sponsorship Proposal Email

With any sponsorship proposal you send, you want to keep it short and succinct while showing interest in the company's product or service. You also need to express how they are going to benefit from exposure your channel.

It's OK to use your own tone of voice but do keep it on the professional side: no cursing, shortcut grammar, etc. The main objective in the first email is to pique your reader's interest rather than have them commit to stuff right away, so save items like prices and technical details until you establish a conversation.

Hi Company_Awesome,

My name's Widgy and I'm the producer of the RealToughGadget channel on YouTube. I'm a big fan of your company -- I actually bought not one, but three of your Handy Dandy Widgets recently: one for my living room and two for my kitchen. The simplicity of the design is awesome and I'm loving the Fantabulous X feature. In fact I did an unboxing video not too long ago: www.youtube.com/HandyDandyWidgetReviewLink

*I use all three of my Handy Dandy Widgets daily and I'm writing today to ask if you'd like to partner with me for a sponsorship. Your product has a lot of potential with my audience and it would be a perfect opportunity to get the Widget in front of hundreds [***or thousands, depending on your sub/watch counts***] of people who care.*

My channel focuses exclusively on Widgets and I know the Handy

Dandy Widget is going to get my audience excited, especially when they see an in-depth demo of it.

I would love to hear your thoughts on this opportunity. I can also be reached at 555-555-5555.

Thanks for reading and I'm looking forward to hearing from you!
-Widgy

Printed in Poland
by Amazon Fulfillment
Poland Sp. z o.o., Wrocław